Music for a Summer's Evening

Music for a Summer's Evening

Music for a Summer's Evening carries us in sound from cherry blossom time in Japan to the orange groves of Florida, from the tranquility of rural France to the exotic delights of Moorish Spain. It brings us great orchestras and voices, the seductive charm of the piano, the haunting strains of the classical guitar, the sparkle of the solo violin. There is the genius of Mozart, Chopin, Puccini, Gershwin, and many more. Sit back, relax, and let the music transport you to a magical world of refreshing breezes and timeless pleasures.

THE LISTENER'S GUIDE — WHAT THE SYMBOLS MEAN

THE COMPOSERS
Their lives... their loves.. their legacies...

THE MUSIC
Explanation... analysis... interpretation...

THE INSPIRATION
How works of genius came to be written

THE BACKGROUND
People, places, and events linked to the music

Contents

WOLFGANG AMADEUS MOZART *1756-1791*

Eine kleine Nachtmusik

K525, FIRST MOVEMENT

Above: *Vienna's Schönbrunn Palace was a typical venue for performances of Mozart's "background" music.* Inset: *The composer, age 14.*

The German title *Eine kleine Nachtmusik* means "A Little Night Music," which is another way of saying a "serenade." Eighteenth-century composers wrote hundreds of such pieces, as background music to royal and other aristocratic occasions, such as banquets, weddings, or for garden parties held on the palace grounds on warm summer evenings. So a piece like *Eine kleine Nachtmusik*—despite its brisk opening bars that seem to be saying "Sit up and listen to this!"—was not intended for the formal atmosphere of the concert hall. Enjoying the music while relaxing at home is more like what Mozart had in mind.

A TALENT TO AMAZE

Stories of Mozart's amazing abilities as a child prodigy abound, and most of them are true. When he was only 6 years old, he gave a harpsichord recital with the keyboard covered by a cloth so that he could not see the keys. Mozart was note-perfect in every piece!

FRINGE MUSICIANS

Eine kleine Nachtmusik is usually played today by a small string orchestra. But Mozart originally wrote it for a string quintet of two violins, viola, cello, and double bass—easy to accommodate in the corner of a banquet room, ballroom, or terrace, where the musicians would be neither too conspicuous nor underfoot.

DR. KÖCHEL'S FAMOUS CATALOG

The "K" number placed after the title of Mozart's compositions refers to the 19th-century Austrian scholar Ludwig Köchel (pronounced "kur-kel"), who listed numerically all Mozart's works in what he believed to be the order of their composition. Dr. Köchel had access to the composer's personal record *(right)*. The catalog opens (K1) with a harpsichord minuet that Mozart probably wrote in December 1761, when he was not yet 6 years old! Last in the catalog is the unfinished *Requiem Mass* (K626).

KEY NOTES

Mozart wrote another serenade called the Serenata Notturna *(K239), which in Italian means almost exactly the same thing as* Eine kleine Nachtmusik.

FREDERICK DELIUS
1862-1934

Koanga

LA CALINDA

La Calinda is the name of a dance that was once popular among West African slaves working on the sugar plantations of the Caribbean islands. Delius's use of this gentle but persistent rhythm, rising to a climax and dying away again, conjures up a picture of tropical warmth and color. The piece comes from Delius's opera *Koanga*, whose story, like that of Gershwin's *Porgy and Bess*, is about a black community that grew up around old plantations. Koanga, an enslaved African chieftain, escapes from his masters and uses voodoo rites to exact his revenge, before dying with Palmyra, the woman who loves him.

THE SOUNDS OF THE SOUTH

As a young man, the English composer Frederick Delius, anxious to get away from the family manufacturing business in Yorkshire, managed an orange grove in Florida. It was there that he heard and came to love the old, Caribbean-style songs and dances, whose melodies and rhythms had a profound influence on his own music.

EXILE AND THE CONDUCTOR

Delius never much liked England, the land of his birth. After his early travels in America, the composer  lived for much of the rest of his life in a village near Fontainebleau, a little way south of Paris. But it was an Englishman who became his greatest champion. The celebrated conductor Sir Thomas Beecham gave the first performance of many of Delius's works, and recorded most of his music. Upon the composer's death, it was Beecham who arranged for him to be buried in a quiet English churchyard.

Delius's champion Sir Thomas Beecham was a favorite subject of British cartoonists.

TALENT UNDIMMED

Delius was blind and paralyzed in middle age, the result of syphilis. His mind, however, was unaffected, and he completed his last compositions with the help of his devoted assistant, fellow Englishman Eric Fenby. These are among the composer's finest works.

KEY NOTES

Inspired by his experiences in the United States, the expatriate Englishman Frederick Delius composed his Florida Suite *and* Appalachia *for voices and orchestra.*

5

FRÉDÉRIC CHOPIN *1810-1849*

Nocturne in E-flat Major

OPUS 9 NO.2

The word "nocturne" means "night piece," music that is quiet and pensive in mood. Chopin wrote 21 nocturnes in total. This one, composed when he was barely out of his teens, is the best loved of all. The long melody unfolds into a mood of dreamy contemplation. Chopin adds some wonderfully decorative notes toward the end, which may suggest the shimmer of moonlight, before the nocturne ends as quietly and serenely as it began.

Chopin, by the celebrated French artist Eugène Delacroix (1798-1863).

MUSICAL MELTING POT

Chopin was born in Poland, and he always looked upon that country as his homeland. But his father was a Frenchman, and the restless young composer settled in France when he was 21. Musically, Chopin's style of composition is firmly in the French tradition of keyboard music, but he proclaimed his love for his native land in his *mazurkas* (Polish folk dances) and *polonaises* (Polish processional dances).

CHOPIN'S GREAT LOVE

Chopin had a celebrated love affair with the French writer George Sand (1804-76). This extraordinary woman's real name was Aurore Dudevant, and her choice of a male pseudonym combined with her numerous affairs with famous men made her a figure of worldwide interest and notoriety. In fact, she was almost motherly in her relationship with Chopin, which began in 1838 and lasted for eight years. During the winter of 1838-9, the couple and Sand's two children stayed on the Mediterranean island of Majorca, hoping this would be good for the composer's already fragile health. Unhappily, the weather turned cold and wet, and Chopin returned to France a very sick man, probably suffering from the tuberculosis that would cut his life tragically short.

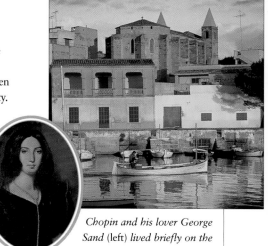

Chopin and his lover George Sand (left) *lived briefly on the island of Majorca* (above).

THE IRISH CONNECTION

Although Chopin's nocturnes are the ones that most people know, he was not the first composer to write this type of dreamy piano music. The credit for that is usually given to the Irish pianist and composer John Field (1782-1837). Field first worked for the London-based composer and piano-maker Muzio Clementi, traveling around Europe demonstrating Clementi's pianos. Field then settled in St. Petersburg, where he pursued his career as a concert pianist and composed the original nocturnes.

KEY NOTES

Chopin wrote two piano concertos (pieces for at least one soloist and an orchestra), which he played on his infrequent but popular concert tours. Otherwise, nearly everything else he composed was for the piano alone. No other great composer has written so much music for just one instrument.

Oberon and Titania, King and Queen of the Fairies, are surrounded by adoring subjects in this painting of the magical world of A Midsummer Night's Dream.

FELIX MENDELSSOHN *1809-1847*

A Midsummer Night's Dream

OVERTURE

The four hushed chords on flutes, oboes, clarinets, and bassoons at the beginning of this piece are among the most magical in all music. They raise the curtain on the glorious fantasy world of Shakespeare's play. When the chords return at the end, as the music trails away, they leave a memory of this most beautiful of dreams for a midsummer's night. Many years later, Mendelssohn wrote more music for the same play, including the famous "Wedding March"—but nothing that surpasses this wonderfully evocative overture.

THE CHILD PRODIGY

Mendelssohn was only 17 when he composed this masterpiece. By then, he was already a seasoned composer. Encouraged by his family and teachers, the precocious Felix began writing music when he was 9 or 10 years old. And the year before his *Midsummer Night's Dream* Overture, Mendelssohn composed another extraordinary work for one so young, the lovely *Octet for Strings*.

Felix Mendelssohn age 13.

MENDELSSOHN'S MUSICAL DONKEY

The Overture is full of musical descriptions. The most vivid of these is inspired by the moment in the play when the fairy messenger Puck turns Bottom the Weaver into an ass. Heavy, repeated notes on horns, cellos, basses, and kettledrum are followed by a little skipping tune on violins and clarinet, then by the unmistakable braying of a donkey (*right*). Many other composers, such as Haydn, Beethoven, and Richard Strauss, also imitated animal sounds in their music. But, for sheer zest and joy, nothing beats this example by Mendelssohn.

A SOUND FROM THE PAST

Mendelssohn's original score for the Overture includes a part for the ophicleide (pronounced "offi" as in "office"–"Clyde"), a brass instrument with a sound similar to that of a tuba. It is now almost forgotten, but Berlioz, Wagner, and Verdi all wrote for the ophicleide, and it was also once popular in military bands.

Brass ophicleide, circa 1810

Shakespeare in Music

Mendelssohn was one of many composers who have found Shakespeare's plays a source of inspiration. This was particularly the case with the 19th-century Romantic composers: Berlioz's dramatic symphony *Romeo and Juliet*; Liszt's symphonic poem *Hamlet*; Nicolai's opera *The Merry Wives of Windsor*; Tchaikovsky's fantasy overtures *Romeo and Juliet*, *Hamlet*, and *The Tempest*; Verdi's great operas *Macbeth*, *Otello*, and *Falstaff*. Twentieth-century examples include Samuel Barber's opera *Antony and Cleopatra* and Benjamin Britten's celebrated *A Midsummer Night's Dream*.

This statue of England's greatest poet and playwright was erected in 1904 in Weimar, Germany.

Composer at Court

The music to *A Midsummer Night's Dream* was only the start of Mendelssohn's romance with England. He made several visits to the British Isles, where his music was perhaps even more popular than it was in his native Germany. Mendelssohn was the favorite composer of Queen Victoria and Prince Albert, and was frequently their guest at Buckingham Palace and Windsor Castle *(above)*.

KEY NOTES

Mendelssohn's sister Fanny was also a talented composer. But her work was not publicly performed because a musical career was not thought proper for women then.

ALEKSANDR BORODIN *1833-1887*

Prince Igor

POLOVSTIAN DANCES, MAIDENS' DANCE

At this juncture in the opera, the Prince has been captured by the Polovtsi, a tribe of Asiatic warrior horsemen. Their chieftain entertains his royal prisoner with a spectacular program of songs and dances—the *Polovtsian Dances*—including the ravishing "Maidens' Dance."

The famous 1950s stage and screen musical *Kismet* made use of Borodin's music. The smash hit from this show—and one of the greatest hits of the decade—was "A Stranger in Paradise." The tune for this was lifted straight from the "Maidens' Dance."

A GIFTED AMATEUR

Borodin was a professional chemist, not a professional musician. Often, he only had time to compose when he was ill. In fact, friends anxious for his music used to greet him with the words, "I hope you're not feeling well!" Borodin died without finishing *Prince Igor*, and it was prepared for performance by Rimsky-Korsakov and Glazunov.

KEY NOTES

Borodin also wrote a very descriptive piece for the orchestra called In the Steppes of Central Asia, *which echoes the plod of camels crossing the desert.*

GEORGE GERSHWIN *1898-1937*

Porgy and Bess

SUMMERTIME

George Gershwin's opera *Porgy and Bess* is set in and around Catfish Row, a tumbledown waterfront tenement in Charleston, South Carolina. Porgy kills the brutal stevedore Crown for the love of Bess. Bess is then lured to New York by an evil man named Sportin' Life, but Porgy follows, determined to save her.

The opera is not as grim as such a description suggests, and in both music and action Gershwin brilliantly evokes the poignancy of the characters. "Summertime" is a lullaby, sung as night descends on Catfish Row. With a hint of the "blues," Gershwin conjures up the heavy summer heat and lazy days of the old Southern port.

THE MASTER ARRANGER

This "Symphonic Suite" of the music from *Porgy and Bess* was written by Robert Russell Bennett (1894-1981). He orchestrated or made arrangements of music for a host of great American stage and screen musical shows, including *Show Boat, Oklahoma!, Carousel, Annie Get Your Gun, South Pacific, Kiss Me Kate, The King and I,* and *The Sound of Music.*

TOAST OF THE TOWN

George Gershwin's career was one of the great American success stories. Born in Brooklyn, New York, to poor Russian-Jewish immigrants, he began playing the piano in Tin Pan Alley, New York's old music publishing district, at the age of 16. With his older brother Ira writing lyrics for many of his songs, George soon became one of the most successful composers for the Broadway stage and then Hollywood. At the same time Gershwin recognized ragtime and blues as America's own folk music. In *Rhapsody in Blue,* he was the first to bring such rhythms into the concert hall, and, with *Porgy and Bess,* into the opera house. Gershwin accomplished all this and more before his tragic death at 39.

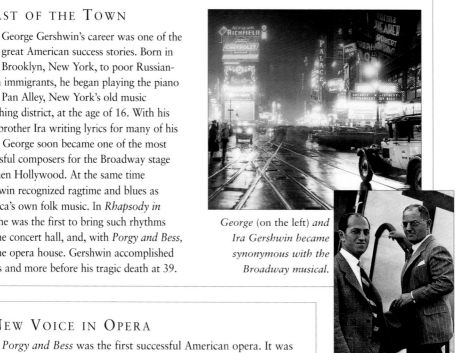

George (on the left) *and Ira Gershwin became synonymous with the Broadway musical.*

A NEW VOICE IN OPERA

Porgy and Bess was the first successful American opera. It was also the first opera with an all-black cast, inspired by black folk music—gospel, blues, and the increasingly popular jazz. The author of the play on which it is based, Du Bose Heyward, lived in Charleston himself. When Gershwin came to write the music, he rented a beach house in Heyward's neighborhood and became involved in the lives of his neighbors, including attending the local churches, where he became familiar with the exuberance and joy of gospel music.

KEY NOTES

"Summertime" is an enduring favorite from **Porgy and Bess.** Equally memorable is "It Ain't Necessarily So."

ANTONIO VIVALDI *1678-1741*

The Four Seasons

SUMMER

V ivaldi's summer is a tempestuous one! To spell out what the music is depicting, the composer accompanies his music with lines of verse. First there is sultry heat, then the call of the cuckoo, followed by sudden and ominous gusts of wind. For the middle section of the work, the poem describes a shepherd boy frightened by flashes of lightning and tormented by swarms of gnats and flies. Finally, thunder cracks and rumbles while hail and rain beat down on the fields of corn. Vivaldi marvelously captures all these moods and impressions with just a small orchestra of violins, violas, and cellos, and a part for solo violin.

A SIGN OF THE TIMES

In Vivaldi's lifetime, works such as *The Four Seasons* were performed with a *continuo* part. This might be played on a double bass, organ, or harpsichord. The continuo player usually followed the bass or bottom line of the harmony. His role was to keep the rest of the orchestra playing together, in the days before there were such people as conductors to direct a performance from the podium!

THE RED PRIEST

Antonio Vivaldi was one of the greatest composers of the Baroque period, which lasted from about 1600 to 1750. An ordained priest with striking red hair, Vivaldi was nicknamed "the Red Priest." He was noted for the infrequency with which he celebrated mass; his enemies attributed this to an allegedly debauched lifestyle. Vivaldi had an innocent explanation—he claimed that the incense aggravated his asthma.

For many years, Vivaldi taught music at a girls' orphanage in his native city of Venice, and music-lovers came from all over Europe to hear the excellent girls' orchestra that he trained and directed.

Eighteenth-century Venice was home to Vivaldi and his famous girls' orchestra.

PAINTING PICTURES WITH MUSIC

The opening lines of Vivaldi's poem speak of the baking sun that exhausts man and beast, and makes the pine trees burn. The weak, broken-up little phrases of the music perfectly echo this sense of oppressive heat. This piece is a fine example of "program music," which is music intended to make the listener visualize a scene, or experience a feeling. Program music is quite different from "incidental music," the sort written for movies and television. Incidental music is meant to reinforce the screen images it accompanies. Program music is designed to do the job entirely on its own.

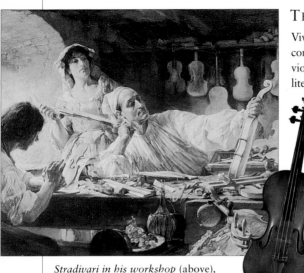

Stradivari in his workshop (above),
and one of his famous creations (inset).

THE ITALIAN CRAFT

Vivaldi's *The Four Seasons* are four concertos for string orchestra and solo violin. The Italian word *concerto* literally means "playing together." Italy was the birthplace of the concerto, especially for stringed instruments. This was largely because Italy, during the 17th and 18th centuries, led the way in the design and construction of violins, violas, and cellos. Nearly all the great instrument-makers lived and worked in the town of Cremona, near Milan. The most famous of them was Antonio Stradivari (1644-1737), whose name is sometimes given the Latin spelling of Stradivarius.

VIVALDI'S ENDURING APPEAL

Among Vivaldi's contemporaries, one of his biggest admirers was J. S. Bach. Bach paid Vivaldi the great compliment of arranging several of his string concertos for other instruments, the most famous of these being the *Concerto for Four Harpsichords and Strings* (taken from Vivaldi's set of 12 concertos published as his Opus 3). But it was *The Four Seasons*, belonging to the set published as Opus 8, that made Vivaldi's name recognized around the world.

KEY NOTES

The four concertos that make up The Four Seasons *belong to a larger group of concertos, all of which are combined under the title* The Contest between Harmony and Invention.

CLAUDE DEBUSSY *1862-1918*

The Girl with the Flaxen Hair

*L*a Fille aux cheveux de lin ("The Girl with the Flaxen Hair") is one of the most charming pieces from Debussy's collection of piano preludes. It was probably inspired by a poem about a lovely young girl with light blond hair and rosy red lips wandering through a field of clover, singing softly to herself. The tender opening melody and Debussy's shifting harmonies also suggest the drowsy warmth and light of a perfect summer's day.

KEY NOTES

Another of Debussy's piano preludes is titled "Feux d'artifice" ("Fireworks"). It ends with a snatch of "La Marseillaise", the French national anthem. There are always fireworks on Bastille Day (July 14), France's great national holiday.

THE PAINTERLY COMPOSER

Debussy's piano preludes are not a "prelude" to anything, but self-contained pieces. Nearly all of them evoke some scene or mood, from the sparkle of sunlight on water to wind and snow. His music is often compared with the paintings of Manet, Monet *(above)*, and other French Impressionists.

GIACOMO PUCCINI *1858-1924*

Madame Butterfly

HUMMING CHORUS

A Japanese geisha girl, Cio Cio San (Madame Butterfly), marries the handsome young American naval officer Lt. Pinkerton during his shore leave in Nagasaki. After a brief honeymoon, Pinkerton leaves on his warship, unaware that his bride is pregnant. Three years pass. Everyone tells Butterfly that her husband has abandoned her and their infant son. She refuses to believe this, and to her great joy, Pinkerton's ship does return to Nagasaki. Butterfly decorates her little home overlooking the harbor with cherry blossom and waits expectantly for her husband as night falls. This lovely "Humming Chorus" (sung offstage) accompanies her vigil beneath a starry sky.

Butterfly and her faithful maid Suzuki peer out into the night-lit harbor, awaiting the arrival of Pinkerton.

OPENING-NIGHT FIASCO

The premiere of *Madame Butterfly* at La Scala in Milan was a disaster, largely because Puccini's rivals organized a hostile "claque"— a group of people hired to boo and hiss. But things turned out for the best. Puccini made improvements to his opera, which then became a huge hit. He bought a yacht, which he named *Cio Cio San* after his tragic heroine.

EAST MEETS WEST

In July 1853, Commodore Perry of the U.S. Navy sailed a squadron of warships into the Japanese harbor of Uraga and forcibly opened Japan up to the rest of the world. This ended more than two centuries of self-imposed isolation by that mysterious nation. Among other cultural shocks, the incursion led to countless liaisons between Japanese geisha girls and American sailors.

Above: *A Japanese woodblock print depicting Commodore Perry's arrival in Uraga in 1853.*
Inset: *A typical geisha girl of the Butterfly era.*

THE REAL BUTTERFLY

The story of *Madame Butterfly* is based on historical fact. Puccini took the idea and the title for his opera from a play by the dramatist David Belasco. Belasco, in turn, based his play on a magazine article, recounting the sad story of a real-life geisha girl, Tsuru Yamamura, who was jilted by her American sailor husband and tried to take her own life. In Puccini's opera, poor Butterfly does finally kill herself.

KEY NOTES

The most famous aria in Madame Butterfly *is "Un bel di," in which Cio Cio San declares that "One fine day," her American husband, Lt. Pinkerton, will return to her and their little son.*

FRANCISCO TÁRREGA *1852-1909*

Memories of the Alhambra

The Alhambra, just outside the city of Granada in Spain, was the 12th-century palace of the Moorish kings. A place of majestic walls and towers and such treasures as the alabaster fountain in the Court of Lions, the Alhambra stands amid subtropical gardens with the snow-capped mountains of the Sierra Nevada in the distance. Tárrega evokes all the light and shade, and the cool splash of water, of this architectural masterpiece. He does so with a single guitar and a lazy melody played with a rapid *(tremolo)* plucking action by the guitarist.

The gardens of the Alhambra are unsurpassed as an oasis of peace and tranquility.

CLASSICAL REVIVAL

The Spanish composer Francisco Tárrega pioneered a revival of interest in the Spanish, or Classical, guitar after a long period of neglect. He gave recitals in Paris, London, and other big European cities, and became known as "the Sarasate of the guitar." (Pablo Sarasate was a celebrated Spanish violinist.) *Recuerdos de la Alhambra (Memories of the Alhambra)* is his best-known composition. Tárrega also transcribed for the guitar many pieces by other Spanish composers, including his friends Albéniz and Granados.

LEGACY OF THE MOORS

The Moors left far more than fabulous architecture as a reminder of their presence in Spain. For example, the ancestor of the modern guitar was another plucked stringed instrument, the *vihuela de mano*. This, in turn, can be traced back to the types of stringed instrument played by the Arabs and Moors of North Africa *(left, a current example)*.

AN AMERICAN IN SPAIN

The writer Washington Irving (1783-1859) created such enduring characters in American literature as Rip Van Winkle and the Headless Horseman. Irving lived in Spain for a time, and researched the history of

Washington Irving

the North African Moors, who invaded and occupied most of Spain for several hundred years beginning in the 8th century. Irving wrote two important books on the subject, *The Conquest of Granada* and *Tales of the Alhambra*.

KEY NOTES

Another of Tárrega's guitar pieces is "Capricho árabe" ("Arabic Caprice").

MARIE JOSEPH CANTELOUBE *1879-1957*

Songs of the Auvergne
BAÏLÈRO

The Auvergne region of France is a high plateau with extinct volcanoes and green, rolling hills stretching as far as the eye can see. Under summer skies, it is a land of skylarks, butterflies, and lush carpets of wildflowers. This all comes across in the lilting strains of the folk song "Baïlèro", a shepherd's call in the Auvergne dialect arranged by the French composer Marie Joseph Canteloube. The orchestral accompaniment, with its lovely, echoing phrases on oboe and flute, adds the finishing touches to a glorious landscape picture.

Folk Song Collecting

Canteloube's collection of old folk songs from the Auvergne was part of a much wider interest in folk music among 20th-century composers and musicians. They were anxious to make collections of such music before it was forgotten and lost forever. Canteloube's contemporaries, Australian-born Percy Grainger and British composer Ralph Vaughan Williams, were doing much the same thing in England. So were Béla Bartók and Zoltán Kodály in Hungary and neighboring Transylvania. In America, in a distinguished line running from Stephen Foster to Aaron Copland, composers were keenly interested in old hymns, dances, and songs, from the Appalachian Mountains to the prairies.

Appalachian music-makers during the 1920s—a rich source for collectors of authentic folk music.

The Sound of Pipes

Canteloube's beautiful arrangements are the work of a professional musician. The songs he collected and arranged would probably have been sung to a set of shepherd's bagpipes. Today, people think of bagpipes as being a specifically Scottish instrument. In fact, various types of bagpipes have been played all over the Middle East and Europe, going back in history to well before the Christian era.

KEY NOTES

Canteloube arranged other songs in the age-old and strange-sounding Auvergne dialect, including "L'Aio dè rotso" ("Spring Water"); "Passo pel prat" ("Over the Meadow"); and "Ound onorèn gorda?" ("Where Shall We Go to Graze?")

LUDWIG VAN BEETHOVEN *1770-1827*

Symphony No. 6 in F Major

OPUS 68 (PASTORAL), FIFTH MOVEMENT

The descriptive title to this movement is "Shepherd's Song: Happy and Thankful Feelings after the Storm." The piece opens as the storm rumbles away into the distance. Horns and woodwind call to each other on three notes; these notes turn into the lovely, melodic theme that runs through the rest of the movement. A rainbow arching across the sky, fading sunlight, and the shadows of evening gradually lengthening over the woods and fields are all suggested by this wonderful music.

ALONE WITH NATURE

Beethoven always loved the countryside. He often walked for hours over the fields and hills around Vienna, composing music in his mind. Many 19th-century composers were inspired by scenes taken from nature—mountains, rivers, waterfalls, wind, rain, snow, the ocean. Beethoven was the first and foremost of these. Perhaps understandably, as his deafness grew worse, the great composer seemed increasingly to prefer communing with nature over grappling with the immense problems of human communication.

Above: *Beethoven sought solace from his deafness in the countryside.* Inset: *The composer's ear trumpet, resting on a manuscript.*

MUSICAL REVOLUTION

Beethoven's *Pastoral* Symphony was just as revolutionary in its day as many of his other works. Composers before Beethoven— notably Vivaldi—had written descriptive music. But this was the first symphony with such a clearly detailed pictorial "program;" each of its five movements depicting a particular mood, scene, or event. Also, this was the first major symphony to have five movements instead of the conventional four. And perhaps most important, the last three movements run on without a break—a true revolution in the symphonic form.

KEY NOTES

The program titles of the other four movements of Beethoven's evocative Pastoral Symphony *are:*
"Awakening of Happy Feelings on Arriving in the Country";
"By the Brook";
"Happy Gathering of Country Folk";
and "Storm".

Credits & Acknowledgments